TREASURES
TO
SEE

TREASURES TO SEE

A Museum Picture-Book
by Leonard Weisgard

NEW YORK

HARCOURT, BRACE AND COMPANY

ALL over the world, wherever you may be, you will find museums.
There are museums of natural history,
museums of science and industry,
museums of cities,
museums of cars.
There is even a museum of baseball.

Up these stairs, through these doors,
there is still another kind of museum—
a museum of art.

Long, long ago, men started to make tools
and weapons.
Then some began to paint and draw pictures.
Others made clothing, and still others jewelry.
There were some who made furniture,
and others who built houses.
Wonderful things were created,
many of which we can still see today.

Here, in this museum with its many vast rooms,
are some of these wonderful things for us to see
and enjoy, works of art from ancient to modern
times, collected from all parts of the world.

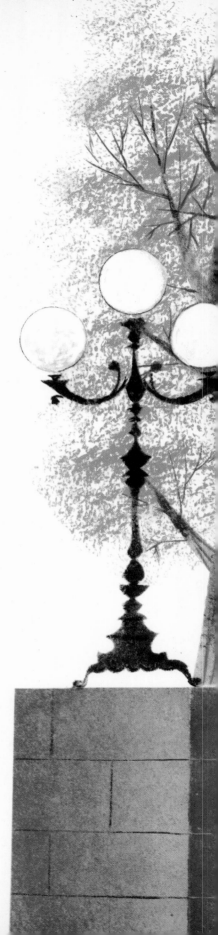

In the Egyptian rooms you will find statues of gods and kings and queens with unusual headdresses, interesting jewelry of gold and precious gems, and figures of the Egyptian people of ancient times carved from wood and stone or painted on walls.

The carved figures, painted in brilliant colors, show people who lived a long time ago in Egypt, bearing gifts for the gods or performing some simple act of their daily lives. The wall paintings are of people at work, or farming, hunting, fishing, even looking for birds on the river.

The Goddess Hat-Hor, 1411-1375 B.C. (crystalline rock)
Painting on wall of tomb
Painted wooden figure of girl carrying offerings of food,
    about 2000 B.C.

Walking through castle-like
halls built of stone, you
will come to the galleries
of armor. Under arches and
vaulted ceilings, the light
from great stained glass
windows shines down on
parades of knights in armor.
And tapestries, woven in
medieval times, show the
way in which the people
dressed and lived, scenes
from their legends and stories,
their games, and how they
hunted and did battle.

Stained glass windows, *The Apostles*, at Bourges Cathedral,
    France, 12th century
Monument of *Gattamelata* by Donatello, 1386-1466,
    Padua, Italy (bronze)
Franco-Flemish tapestry, *The Unicorn in Captivity*, about 1514
Armor of George Clifford, Third Earl of Cumberland, English, 1590

Here, also, beneath a pageantry of ancient banners, battle standards, and flags and pennants that hang from the walls and ceiling, are displays of medieval weapons carried by knights and their henchmen. There are steel cutlasses, sharp curved sabers, court swords, tilting lances, and great shields. Here, too, are all kinds of heavy armor worn by horses, as well as men, in battle or in jousting tournaments.

Banner (Anglo-Saxon), Edward the Confessor, 1002?-1066
Helmet (Saxon), 1590
Shield (French), Louis XIV, 1643-1715
Halberds (Polish), 17th century
Horse armor, Carlos V (Charles I of Spain), 1520-1556
Helmet, basket-hilted sword, mace, breastplate (European), about 1500

In the sculpture galleries
you will see statues of
animals, gods, kings and
queens, of saints and men,
of women and children.
Some pieces were made
thousands of years ago;
some were created yesterday.

David by Andrea del Verrocchio (Italian),
    1435-1488 (bronze)
Figure from the tomb of Lorenzo de' Medici
    by Michelangelo (Italian), 1475-1564
Saint George by Donatello (Italian),
    1386-1466 (marble)
Family group by Henry Moore (English),
    1898-   (bronze)
Madonna and child (French), 13th century
    (painted wood)
Madonna and child by Luca della Robbia (Italian),
    1400-1482 (enameled terra cotta)

Men have carved statues out of wood, chipped them from stone, modeled them of clay and plaster, or molded them in metal, gold, silver, bronze, or copper.

Throughout the ages, people have used sculptured figures in churches, in public squares, buildings, and parks, and in their homes and gardens, to worship their gods, to honor important men and women, to add beauty everywhere.

Winged Victory of Samothrace (Greek), about 305 B.C. (marble)
Mother and child, Henry Moore (English), 1898-
Colossal head of a warrior (Etruscan), about 500 B.C.

On the walls of the painting galleries
hang pictures created by great artists
of the many nations of the world.
Each artist, working in his own
particular way, has painted a picture
that lives for us on wood, canvas,
paper, or even on part of a wall.

The Syndics of the Amsterdam Cloth Guild by Rembrandt van Rijn
　(Dutch School), 1606-1669
Vrouw Bodolphe by Frans Hals (Dutch School), 1580?-1666
Don Manuel Osorio de Zúñiga by Francisco José de Goya y Lucientes
　(Spanish School), 1746-1828
View of Toledo by El Greco (Spanish School), 1541-1614

Besides painting in oils,
artists also work in pastels,
using soft chalks, make wash
drawings with water colors,
or create exciting sketches
with pencil or pen and ink.
Others work on metal or wood
to make etchings or engravings.
These pictures on wood or metal
can be transferred onto paper,
making it possible to produce
many prints of the same picture.

Here in this museum you will see the
magnificent variety of the artists' work.

Through the years master craftsmen and designers have planned public buildings, palaces, and homes, and decorated them in new and interesting ways. The furniture rooms of the museums and the halls of architecture show the great changes in style that have taken place, from time to time, in the home and building arts.

Here you will see such things as pottery stoves, some elegant and tall, decorated with gold, some small and primitive, with carved figures, and beds as they were made hundreds of years ago, ornately carved, draped with rich fabrics.

Porcelain stove, Bavaria, 19th century
Carved and inlaid walnut chair from the Strozzi Palace, Florence, Italy, late 15th century
Carved oak Elizabethan bed from Cumnor Palace, Berkshire, England, 16th century

In the museum you will find whole rooms devoted to ceramics and household utensils. There are vases and glassware, bowls, urns, goblets, pitchers, and domestic objects used by all sorts of people everywhere, long, long ago and today.

When the artist-craftsman was making something for daily use, he often made it good to look at as well as useful. Because of this, many things have been saved for the sake of their beauty, and we, too, can now enjoy them in the museum.

The Departing Warrior vase (Greek), about 440-430 B.C.
The Rospigliosi Cup, to hold salt, attributed to Benvenuto Cellini (Italian), 1500-1571
Amber sugar bowl, Ohio (probably Zanesville), early 19th century
Creamer, 19th century (of Lowestoft ware type)

The arts and crafts of the Far Eastern countries are shown in another room. Here you will see Chinese sculpture, Japanese painting on silk and wood-block prints, ancient Persian and Indian book illustration.

These wonderful things show us how people lived years and years ago on the other side of the world from us.

Portrait of Minamoto-no-Yoritomo ascribed to Fujiwara-no-Takanobu
    (Japanese), Kamakura period, late 12th century (painting on silk)
Painted bowl (Persian), Sultanabad district, 14th century
Equestrian portrait of Aurangzib (Indian), Mughal School, 1658-1707
The Mishima Pass by Katsushika Hokusai (Japanese), 1760-1849 (print)
Statue of horse (Chinese), T'ang Dynasty, 618-907

Just as we dress differently for different seasons or climates, so people have dressed in various ways in other places and times gone by. What they wore may be seen in the costume section of the museum. Our clothes today are still influenced by these old styles.

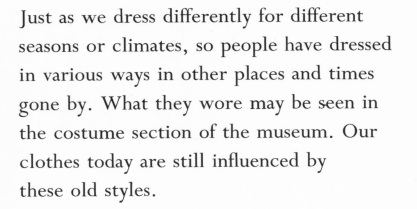

English costume, 1790
French costume, 1690
French costume, beginning of 17th century
German costume, first half of 15th century
French costume, about 1400

Grecian dress, 400-300 B.C.
French dress, 15th century
English dress, about 1776
French dress, about 1778

Now come into the American wing of the museum, where you will find things made by the people who first settled this country.

They needed shelter, so they built homes.

They needed furniture, so they designed their own. And though their needs were quickly met by simply made things, their designs were good. Often, too, they used gay color in decorative patterns, like the folk arts of their homelands, and what they made is pleasing to the eye.

Here are rooms exactly as they were in George Washington's time. Here, too, are primitive paintings, tradesmen's signs, and emblems of unity and freedom that represent the first years of America's history.

New England Queen Anne style chair, 18th century
Cigar-store Indian shop sign, about 1850
Silhouette portrait of Washington by Samuel Folwell, 1765-1813
Type of doorway used in 1707 at Deerfield, Massachusetts
Primitive painting of Mary Childs by Joseph W. Stock, mid-19th century (oil on canvas)
Sgraffito or scratch-decorated plate of Pennsylvania pottery, about 1810
Comb-back Windsor writing chair, about 1775

Because a museum of art is such a big, exciting place, with so many rooms and galleries, you cannot see it all at one time, but you will want to go back again and again.

No matter how often you visit a museum, no matter how much you see each time, there are always new and exciting treasures to discover, more wonderful things to see.

Wood engraving (German), 15th century
Slip-ware platter (Pennsylvania Dutch), 18th century
Rearing Horse by Leonardo da Vinci (Italian), 1452-1519 (bronze)